DOWNLOAD TH

MW00475768

WHEN LIFE
Sucks
RESOURCE KIT

To Get Your FREE Resource Kit Visit:
www.tayamicola.com/resourcekit

READ THIS FIRST

To help you get the most out of this book and turn your life that SUCKS around, I have created a FREE resource kit that you can use while you read.

Visit: www.tayamicola.com/resourcekit

When Life Sucks!

A Therapist's Guide to Surviving and Thriving During Tough Times

Copyright 2016 Taya Micola.
All Rights Reserved.

No part of this book may be reproduced,
distributed, stored in a retrieval system or
transmitted in any form by any electronic,
mechanical, photocopying, recording,
means or otherwise without prior written
permission of the publisher, except in the
case of brief quotations embodied in
reviews and certain other non-commercial
uses permitted by copyright law.

Disclaimer

The information in this book is intended for educational and informational purposes only, and should not be taken as expert instructions or commands. This book does not attempt to replace, nor should it be used as a replacement or substitute for psychological or professional advice. If expert advice or counseling is needed, the services of a competent professional should be sought. The writer cannot be held responsible for its use in particular circumstances, and the writer disclaims responsibility for the book's use in circumstances far from her control.

Table of Contents

Introduction

Chapter 1: I've Got Your Back

Chapter 2: You Have More Skills Than You Realize

Chapter 3: How I Help People

Chapter 4: This Is How You Are Going To Turn Your Life Around

Chapter 5: Let Go Of Things You Cannot Control

Chapter 6: What's Happening Now Isn't Forever.

Chapter 7: Focus On The Outcome.

Chapter 8: Understanding How Your Past Is Still Affecting You

Chapter 9: Is There A Pattern To Your Tough Times?

Chapter 10: What Stage Are You In?

Chapter 11: The Top Emotions That
            Cause Baggage

Chapter 12: Moving Through It And
            Building A Bridge

Chapter 13: Don't Be A Victim, Be A
            Survivor

Chapter 14: Needing Others To Pay

Chapter 15: Plan Your Way Out

Conclusion

Acknowledgements

This book is dedicated to my daughter, Caterina, who has shown us all time and time again that ANYTHING is possible, and that miracles are available and within reach to anyone determined and focused enough to grab them.

If you follow the steps and advice set out in this book not only can you survive the tough times, but you can also find a way to thrive despite it all.

As a counselor who specializes in trauma, I have helped hundreds of people in the last 10 years to heal and overcome the things they've experienced in the past, as well as the things they are currently facing.

In this time, I've seen over and over again that regardless of whether a person is dealing with horrible darkness or just plain awful inconveniences, their ability to heal depends largely on the way they process the sucky-ness.

With the right knowledge, perspective, and willingness to get well again, these clients not only recover, they completely turn their lives around for the better.

In this book I will share with you exactly what has to happen for you to process all that no-good-sucky-bad-stuff in a way that encourages healthy healing and recovery.

Not only that, but if you stick with me, I will also inspire your self-support to rise from within and help you access your inner wisdom to help you make decisions and navigate your way through or over the things that are making your life suck.

You will learn techniques and insights you can begin to use right away to help you powerfully heal and release. Using these techniques and insights will ensure that your life and the situation you are dealing with will improve beyond measure.

By the end of this book, I promise that you will know what you need to know to get over or through the tough times that are making your life suck. You will also know how to build that bridge, how to avoid baggage, AND you will have begun to believe in yourself again and your natural-born ability to conquer. In fact, you may even be feeling more YOU than you've felt in a long time.

Don't disregard the information in this

book. If left unchecked, the psychological trauma that creates a sucky life can leave you struggling with upsetting emotions and create deeper issues for years to come.

Choose to overcome the tough stuff now. By committing to reading and applying the information in this book, you are taking the first step to speeding your recovery today.

While it can take more than reading to prevail over deep feelings, think of this book as an added support, with self-help strategies that can aid in your recovery.

Chapter 1
I've Got Your Back

We don't exactly know each other yet.

But already I am here for you. Before I began writing this book I felt you reach out, and I wanted more than anything to help you even then. Now my words are on the page and all I want to do is wrap you up in them and assure you that you are not alone...

And you're not. Not by a long shot.

You have me for support and you also have **you**.

Me, because I've heard your call and helped others like you who are a bit lost, and *you* because you have been there from the beginning. The you that knows everything about you: your whole story, not just pieces of it. All of it, in every inextricable detail.

While I've helped others with similar stories to heal from similar pain, and while I'm here with my lifeline and this book to pull you from those stormy seas, no one knows your pain quite like you do.

So my first piece of advice to you on this journey is this...

Let me be there for you. Let me help you, share with you and love you — but let **you** be there for you too.

In order for you to get through or over this... **you** need to be on your side. It can't just be me doing everything. It won't work well, and you know it. Now is not the time to turn on yourself.

When life sucks, you can't subscribe to the mentality of "Life sucks and so do I." If you are going to make it through this, if you are going to heal and get over things, the very first thing you must do when life is working against you is to step up and be there for *you*.

No matter what you've been told or led to believe about yourself, the BEST person to support you through this is **you**.

Don't worry. I am here. You have my understanding, my love, and my unending support. But although I am here WITH you, I cannot do this FOR you.

Luckily, you were built for this.

You either simply never realized it or you've somehow forgotten, but that ability is there deep down and we're going to help you fish it out and use it starting right now.

You have a wisdom inside of you that has been taking care of you for all these years. Although I know your life sucks right now and you are hurting, your wisdom is still intact. You may have stopped listening to it, or you may have never really called on it before, but it is there inside of you, nonetheless.

This wisdom can be felt in your loneliest, darkest hours. It's actually there all the time, and you maybe just don't realize.

Some call it intuition, others call it the higher self; some call it the subconscious or your conscience. It's the voice that comes from deep, deep down that carries your wisest self.

We are going to connect with this part of you often and call upon it more frequently. This will be the voice we listen to from now on, not the chaotic, critical, irrational voice that jumps to conclusions and freaks you out with horrible stories and fears.

We need your wisdom to navigate the way.

So can you promise to be there for you? Are you ready to begin finding and using your inner wisdom for the rest of this journey?

Excellent.

Let's assess things. What do you need to DO to support you?

First of all, we need to get you seaworthy. We already have emotional self-support packed and ready (remember — that's the bit where you promised to be there for *you*). Next, we need you to give yourself the support that you need.

We want to sail you right out of your sucky life and into the happy, furthest-thing-from-sucky life that you deserve. Whether you're the tall yacht with exquisite sails and an amazing deck kind of person, or the mahogany jet speed boat with twin turbo engines kind of person, we want you out of these stormy, gloomy, dark and treacherous seas and sailing on beautiful, bright, clear open waters again.

So, about this seaworthy-ness. What do you need in that boat with you to make you shipshape?

Basically, you've already agreed to support yourself emotionally. I'm asking you: what do you need to do to support yourself physically and maybe mentally?

In my opinion, most people who are going through tough times need at least one or all of the following things as a support to get themselves through.

- More sleep
- More exercise/movement
- More time to themselves
- Less time with themselves
- To relax often and deeply
- To release tension
- To think less or get out of their brain
- To eat better

Some of these things may be self-explanatory, but others may give you pause. How do you accomplish these things in a chaotic, overscheduled life?

If you're like many of my clients, you might be exhausted. To support your energy, you might like to consider incorporating a bit of exercise.

Exercise GIVES you energy. It also strengthens you and builds stamina while helping you to release pent-up adrenaline — perfect if your sucky life has you worrying, anxious, or terrified half the time.

Fitness isn't really my thing, but I have found regular exercise to be invaluable when I'm stressed. It has become a key part of my day and my self-support routine.

If joining a gym and working yourself hard for 3 hours every day is your idea of hell, or if it's going to create a stress on your finances, or if it's just not possible with kids etc. — then this is *not* supportive.

It might mean that the best way you can support yourself is to wake up a little earlier and head out for a brisk walk before you start your day. Or perhaps joining a twice-weekly cheap yoga class sounds like a better option. You can even buy yourself a DVD or just walk up and down your stairs if that's all you have time or resources for.

What I'm trying to get across is that it needs to be something that helps you, not something that creates more stress in your life. I guarantee there IS a way for you to give yourself what you need, and in the best and most supportive way that suits your situation.

Look for it. It's out there.

Some other ways to support yourself are:

Do you need to calm your mind? Are you thinking too much and overanalyzing things? Your best form of support might be to meditate.

You can join a class, practice on your own, or download an app on your smart phone. Pick the way that supports you most and do it.

Do you need to have a bit of time on your own? Can you organize someone to take the kids to school one morning a week? Can you ask your boss for a late start on Fridays if you stay late on Thursdays? Can you have lunch away from work instead of at your desk? Can you put the baby in the stroller and go for a walk? By the time you reach that street with your favorite café, the baby's asleep and you've got yourself some 'me' time. Do you see what I'm getting at? There is a way... you just need to find it.

Are you spending too much time on your own, analyzing and catastrophizing? Deep down, do you know that you need to get out more and connect with others? Pull out your calendar, ring some of your most uplifting friends, and plan yourself some fun to look forward to. Then plan to do it all again in a few weeks' time.

If that's too much, then join an online community or create an iMessage group on your phone and start an SMS chat with your friends. Even something as simple as starting a friendly conversation with your neighbor/desk buddy/ stranger on the train can help you get out of your own head and connect with others.

Find a way.

When you've found the right way, things

will get better and your life will stop *sucking* just a little more.

There are some great techniques in this book that can help you with some of these. Use them.

So... what do you need?

Once you've identified this, talk to whomever you need to speak with (your family/partner/friends/boss/roommates/ house-buddies etc. basically whoever you need to get on board) and ask for the support you need. Let them know you're working through some stuff and need help to make it happen.

They may not even have to do very much. Telling them is half the battle. If you say, "I'm going for a walk every morning. It's really important to me," and everyone understands that, they'll leave asking you to do other things until the afternoon. They'll still ask you, but just at a time that suits better. If they don't, train them to.

You need this.

Now don't freak out at this point. Before you slam the book shut and say, "I can't do that, Taya, I can't ask for help," you actually can... but maybe you don't want to.

In my experience, relationships get stronger and people become happier when you let them help you a little.

People like to help.

Think about it. You like helping others—I know you do—and better relationships mean a less sucky life, so do it and be surprised at how much you all benefit.

If you're asking of others, you may inspire them to ask for what they need and again, you will all benefit.

If you're a parent, you will be teaching your children an extremely important skill...to value themselves.

If you are nervous about asking because you don't want to be one of those people who takes others for granted or you don't want to put anybody out, then I can pretty much guarantee you won't be. If you are already conscious of overstepping the mark, you'll never do so.

Besides, you're too awesome for that.

Find a way to make this work, whatever your circumstances, and watch the rewards flow in.

The simple act of self-care is one of the most healing things you can do for yourself.

You have a
wisdom
inside of you
that has been
taking care of
you all these
years. You may
have stopped
listening to it,
or you may
have never
really called
on it before,
but it is there
inside of you,
nonetheless.

Chapter 2
You Have More Skills Than You Realize

You have more skills than you realize, and you're going to need them to get through or over the stuff that's making your life suck.

The number one thing my clients have taught me is that we really can survive anything.

Here they are, broken, torn, and tattered from the horrible things that life or other people have afflicted them with. Some of the things that make their lives suck are a result of others inconsiderate or hurtful actions. Some are the result of bad decisions, and some are sheer bad luck, freak occurrences, or even just some downright frustrating experiences.

31

Yet they all want their lives to not suck.
(Of course they do). They all want to heal
and recover, and again and again, they do.

You can probably imagine that I've heard
many sad, sad stories in the last ten years
I've spent coaching people through or over
tough times. Some stories we can all relate
to, and some are way too sad to share.

Together with my clients, we've faced and
grappled with the darkest sides of
humanity, the cruel actions of others, all
the way through to those very unfair
injustices that life just sometimes bestows
on us.

Tough times come in varying degrees, but
it happens to everyone. No one is immune
to it.

But by helping others clear it and lift it,
I've also seen the most beautiful aspects of
the human spirit. I've witnessed time and
time again the beauty of shedding painful
memories, hurtful events, crippling fears,
and even the petty annoyances, only to
emerge victorious and able to rise above it

all.

I am truly enamored with the resilience and beauty of the human spirit and its amazing ability to triumph.

Of course, I've also had my own personal hell-and-backs. Humdingers, actually, and some of them just recently.

I help people to get over or through the big bad stuff, all the way through to the little insignificant stuff that trips us up and makes life harder than it has to be.

The thing is, it doesn't actually matter if we are talking about bigger issues in your closet or little hiccups from your past. Whether we are talking about heartbreak, pain or health worries, or even just money trouble, all of these, no matter the details, can really strip our self-esteem, make us question our confidence and our worth, and can create fear about them happening again.

That's when we know it's become baggage. And baggage is bad.

Baggage hurts.

It sits deep inside of you like telepathic barbed wire. Why telepathic? Because if someone just mentions something vaguely similar to what your baggage is about, it mentally jabs you and reminds you. In fact, it pokes at you when you're thinking about it, or when you're not thinking about it. It goes to town when something else bad happens to you, and it jabs at you when you're happy, reminding you that you once weren't, and that all of this can be taken away from you again. It robs you of your confidence when you're trying to muster it, and it takes a chip out of it when you've found it again.

Baggage does all this and more in ways that are blindingly obvious to you, and even in sneaky ways you don't even realize.

Baggage makes you feel small, alone, and helpless.
Baggage is heavy, like a little lead shadow that's always in your life, lurking in the

background.

It can make you feel as if you are a good person but the world is a bad place, or it can make you feel that you are a bad person living in a great world that you're not allowed to play in.

And my least favorite:

Baggage stops you from moving forward.

You can't:
- Have that
- Be that
- Do that
- Know that
- Live that

All because of baggage.

Nasty business, baggage, and we're going to make sure you are armed with defense against it.

More on that later but for now,

You want to get over it!

And rightly so, because you're meant to. You are soooo meant to get over and through this.

You have things to do. Special things. Awesome things that only you can do in your own special way.

Of course, you can't do any of these things if you are too busy surviving the past or the evils of right now.

So how is it that some people get over or through tough times and difficult situations fully and with their self-esteem and personal power intact or renewed, while others never truly put themselves back together again?

By the end of this book you will know and will have begun doing exactly what you need to do to get over or through your stuff so that despite what has happened, you can have the chance to thrive again and enjoy a life that doesn't suck.

I'm already ten steps ahead of you because I know something you don't.

I absolutely know 100% that it is possible for you to move past whatever you're going through and be able to live a GREAT life. I also know you can do it without too much struggle. Not only is it possible, it happens all the time.

But how can that be...? Some people have really been through unspeakable things.

I know...Really...I *know*...

But I also know that it doesn't matter what has happened or is happening to make your life suck...you CAN get over it.

You can do this. You were born to survive and thrive every day. In fact, humans are hardwired for survival. Your incredible brain is looking for solutions for you on every level at all times. You are constantly problem solving and seeking solutions. And although you may be aware of some things you can do to get through, your deeper mind knows of many, many more ways that you've maybe never consciously thought of. We are going to get it to gather those resources for you now.

Through all the struggles, my clients have taught me over the years that there really is nothing so big and so bad out there that we cannot recover from. They are a true source of inspiration for me every day, and they've shown me so beautifully how we really can go on and have amazing lives despite painful experiences.

People succeed every day in letting go, moving on, and claiming *their* happily ever after. People get past themselves and life's darker side all the time, and you can too. Once you know the difference between those who *do* move past things and those who don't, once you know the way forward, as long as you keep going in the right direction, you *will* get there.

So while this is just a book, it's also your guide, your map, and your inspiration. Remember, there are people out there with less self-belief, less courage and conviction, and with less support who have gone through much darker things than you've faced or are facing. Yet they have *still* managed to patch themselves up in a way that lets them thrive and achieve all the same things that you yourself want to achieve, and more.

This means you can too. You really, really can.

This book is infused with all the encouragement and information I can give you to help you understand how to be one of those people who does get through and over it.

Before we go any further, you need to remember something. Something important, something that you may have forgotten...

You are incredible!

AND...
You have survived so much already. Think about it...

You HAVE.

This isn't your first rodeo — you've gotten through hard times before, and you've survived. At the very least you've learned to walk, talk, and possibly even fend off siblings. You've survived the first day of school and the first day of high school. We all have, and even though there is more to come, you can make it through.

You really can do this.

Not only that, the Universe wants you to get through this.

You were led to this book because you were asking for help — I know you were. The Universe listened and here we are. Your seeking mechanism in your brain was on fire, and you found this resource and together we are getting you to a better place.

I'll guide you. Together with your commitment to heal and my commitment to help you heal, you will get there. Even if you don't know how yet, even if you can't see an end in sight (yet), you can get there.

You will see, with the right treatment, self-help strategies and support, you really can recover.

Anyone can.

There are lots of ways to help and lots of things you can do.

There are things you can do to help your body, because, let's face it, some of those feelings we feel inside are physically horrendous. There are things you can do to help your mind — because all that thinking, analyzing and even catastrophizing takes it's toll too. There are things you can do for your spirit, because you are so much more than just a brain and a body. You are a being, a being of light that needs to shine.

You have a plan and a purpose for being here, and so your spirit needs help to soar, as well, because when you are soaring and your spirit is healed and healthy, your life is enriched and fulfilling.

Not just for you, but for everybody.

You need you healthy, and so do we. When you are healthy, happy, and soaring, it benefits us all. The whole of mankind and the Universe.

We all want you to heal because it will not only be better for you, but better for us, as well. You'll be happy with your life that doesn't suck and you will be doing great things we can all benefit from.

When you are happy and fulfilled, you are your most amazing version of you. You do great things when you're feeling that good. You work better and you play better. You are happy but you are also inspiring, reminding all of us around you to be OUR best selves. You motivate others just by being your gorgeous, happy self.

This is my favorite version of you. This is the you I want you to be the most. For you...and for all of us.

So let's get cracking...

**You Really
Can Do
This...**

Chapter 3
How I Help People

In my clinic I use the techniques of Kinesiology and Clinical Hypnotherapy.

Kinesiology is a way to move blocks from your energy field. It helps the body to utilize the natural healing mechanism we all have. It is usually a very health-based modality — however, because I am a counselor, I use it to help people find what's blocking them emotionally by very accurately identifying what the emotional stress is behind the problems they face.

Once we find it we can clear it and heal it. It's also great for removing those physical feelings from all the pent-up stress we're carrying about in regards to what is making our life suck.

Clinical Hypnotherapy (not the crazy, silly, 'quack like a duck' kind, but the much more helpful and ethical, "lets explore that on a deeper level" kind) is a fantastic way to utilize the power of your brain to make changes on a deeper level. Although I'm not a neuroscientist, as hypnotherapists we study neuro-psychotherapy and the way our brains naturally think and work to create changes instinctively.

I am also a deeply spiritual and highly intuitive person. Many moons ago, I used to dabble as a psychic, giving readings. I wasn't very good, though, because I spent more time with them talking about their past and feeling their pain instead of focusing on their future. I could see how their baggage was affecting everything. I craved a way to help them release all the things that were keeping them from getting their happily ever after.

So I got myself some amazing new tools. Nowadays, my intuition helps me understand my clients on a deeper level. I feel it, like I've walked the path with them, offering insights to moving forwards.

These three beautiful tools (Kinesiology,

Clinical Hypnotherapy and Intuition) help my clients to work through their stresses quickly, deeply, and with minimal distress.

As we can't exactly have a session together right here in a book, I will be sharing with you some of the tools and discovery methods you can use to help you. These are conveniently bundled for you in the resource kit, which you can download from my website.

Visit www.tayamicola.com/resourcekit.

If you haven't done so already, download it now in preparation.

Of course, there are even more resources out there, but the selection I have included will help you get started and perhaps even lead you down a pathway to uncover more of what you need as you go.

I encourage you to build on them and use them as much as you can, especially during those times when you feel as though you just can't cope.

I'm not just telling you this as a therapist. I've used these same tools in my own life because I have had to get myself through hard times, too, especially recently.

Two years ago my youngest daughter, Caterina, was afflicted with a chronic pain disorder that completely shattered our world. One minute she was fine, and the next she was in crippling pain that went on for months with no reprieve. It was neuropathic pain (nerve pain) deep in her chest wall. Nerve pain is the worst because there is no treatment for it. No painkillers work: not aspirin, not morphine, nothing.

Thank goodness I had a special set of tools that could help when nothing else could. I shudder to think what might have happened if we didn't have those in our arsenal.

She was 9 years old at the time and was living a very full and active life that just stopped in a moment. For the next two years she battled on and off (mostly on) with it.

As a trauma coach, I found my skills

invaluable, but I never thought I would have to use my acute trauma management skills non-stop for two years. For months and months I couldn't work. I could barely leave her to go to the toilet, as some days her pain was unbearable.

Thanks to a great bunch of colleagues, things got much better and we found valuable ways to manage it. She developed many other symptoms and after a million tests they finally came to the conclusion that there was an underlying autoimmune condition, but they didn't know which one.

Although I knew that she could and would heal, her doctors, on the other hand, felt I wasn't accepting things. There were certain symptoms (like the nerve pain) that they felt would be a permanent part of her life. They assured me if the pain went away, it would always come back. We decided as a family that this was unacceptable.

Knowing what I know about trauma and getting your life back on track, we applied all the techniques I'm teaching in this book.

I taught my daughter the importance of self-support. She found she could color and paint to distract herself from the pain. Using her inner wisdom, she found ways to manage and give herself what she needed. She found ways to re-build her life and to be able to complete her schoolwork. She worked *with* her brain through the pain.

My eldest daughter moved out of their shared bedroom for a time, and my husband worked hard to be there for her more, because I simply couldn't be. They and another family friend gave our eldest daughter what she needed when our little family unit couldn't. It wasn't always smooth sailing, but we kept afloat using the principles I'm outlining for you here and in the resource kit.

Everyone supported my morning walk. 20 minutes was all I asked, and amazingly, it restored me for the next 23 hours every single day. It helped me release all the pent-up adrenaline created by the stress of managing a small person with unbearable pain. It gave me time on my own, time I could use to cry, mourn and grieve. Time I could use to still my mind.

Time I could use to connect to my inner wisdom and the love of the Universe. Caterina worked with a colleague of mine, and using hypnotherapy they eliminated her pain completely. She is also 100% symptom free.
Her kidneys are functioning beautifully. Her inflammation has reduced, her immune system is back in a healthy place, and most exciting of all, she looks forward to and enjoys a life that truly doesn't suck.

She is now 11 years old and was declared in remission by her specialist late last year. She is completely symptom free. She feels incredibly confident that the pain will never return, but equally emphatic that if it does, she knows exactly what to do about it.

While we were on that journey we surrounded ourselves with positivity. We watched funny movies. We scoured the Internet for funny cat and parrot memes and videos. We read stories about conquering.

We developed the mindset required to thrive despite the sucky-ness that life had thrown at us.

We downloaded meditations and anything that kept us happy and supported. It worked...all of it worked.

When I shared with my clients the benefits of staying positive during negative times, they cried out for something they could do to stay motivated in positivity and hence this book was born. I've created it for people who are trying to move out of their sucky lives and need support and motivation to stay positive.

Now it's your turn.

Get ready, because in the next chapter we are going to learn the difference between processing things in ways that help you vs. ways that create baggage and stress.

Turn the page and let's get started.

Chapter 4
This Is How You Are Going To Turn Your Life Around.

This is the most important chapter in this book. In this chapter we'll look closely at exactly what you need to do to process things in healthier ways.

In order for you to thrive and then survive the tough times you are dealing with, you need to understand a very important principle. How well you understand and use this principle will determine how successful you will be. It will determine whether you merely survive, or whether you thrive despite the bad stuff...

Are you ready?

It's not what happens… It's how you interpret what happens.

If tough situations happen or come your way, it doesn't matter how they come about or specifically what or how tough it is, exactly. It's how you interpret it that determines how much it will affect you.

Furthermore, how you interpret it basically depends on what you say to yourself about it. So that means, what happens is not as important as the conversations you have with yourself about it.

Even if your tough times involve what someone else does or says, it won't be so much what they do or say that determines how much it makes your life suck. Rather, it matters more what *you* tell yourself about what they've done or said.

If someone at work calls you fat and stupid, there are a few ways you can process that.

1. "They're right, I've been found out, everybody knows my dirty little secret."

This self-talk statement will feed all your insecurities and add to any baggage you already have. It leaves you feeling very disempowered, yet how many of us can relate to it?

2. "I have put on weight, but I'm doing something about it."

This self-talk may touch on one of your insecurities but it will mostly support your decision to continue to lose weight. There's a little disempowerment, but it's quickly regained with the second half of the statement.

3. "Ahh, that's Jo, always quick to put others down. How lonely he must be."

This self-talk feeds no insecurities at all. It neither empowers nor dis-empowers. If anything, it points out the insecurity of others.

In order for you to move through the tough times and be able to let them go, you need to learn to process it in one of the last two ways.

Your self-talk has to support and EMPOWER you in your situation. Anything else creates baggage and makes it harder to get over.

The secret is not in asking you to pretend you aren't affected. That doesn't work. The secret is to react in ways that feel true for you while holding on to your power.

That means that if something bad happens, you can't expect to be like a robot with no feeling. You are allowed to feel the emotions you naturally feel. You can be devastated; in fact, denying you aren't is just kidding yourself. You can be heartbroken, you can be fearful, and you can be disappointed. You can be shocked, hurt, humiliated, and any range of emotions. No one is saying you need to or should deny your emotions.

But watch your self-talk.

Be kind to yourself about it. Have compassion for yourself in those moments. Be a support.

If you find that you are putting yourself down, pick yourself up in the next statement. If you recognize a negative, try to find a positive.

This might mean you have to really change the way you see things.
It might involve changing the way you've always reacted. All are do-able. All will help you.

One of the quickest ways to turn a negative statement around is by using one of these words: OR and BUT.

If you find yourself making a negative statement, add one of these words to the end and quickly turn it around.

OR is a great word to use when you're referring to life. BUT is a great word to use when you're referring to you.

Look at how this simple change can transform a sentence and your thought process.

"I don't think I can afford that phone bill. This is because John left me. I hate that there's never any money anymore..."
BUT...
"I know I WILL get back on my feet. It's only a matter of time."

"I don't think I can afford that phone bill. There's never any money, the bank will probably foreclose, and I'll have to live with my mother."
OR
"It will all be fine. The money could arrive for it tomorrow and I'll be ok...at least I have my mother's place to go to if I ever need it".

Get the picture?

You might be thinking these are pretty generic responses, and you're right. I've chosen easy examples to demonstrate. What if it was a really difficult situation, though?

Jane has just found out John has been cheating on her. When she confronts him, he admits to the affair, saying that he hasn't been happy in a long time and is leaving Jane for the other woman.

Jane is devastated. Nobody expects her not to be.

Here are two examples of split-second thinking:

1. I'm devastated. I'll never get over this. Dammit, this just *proves* all men are bastards. Oh God! (*Remembers that time her mother said, "You always pick the wrong men."*) My mother was right; I always pick the wrong men! I'm so sick of life not turning out for me, but it's always like this.

2. I'm devastated. I'm not sure how I'll get over this. Dammit, *another* man who has let me down. Oh God —

(Remembers that time her mother said, "You always pick the wrong men.") Perhaps she is right and I need to work on that. I want my life to be better.

All the same emotions and memories are acknowledged, but the second one is more supportive and empowering. The emotions and events are being processed in ways that don't create or add emotional baggage. There's a less likely chance of deeper issues developing.

Can you see now what our self-talk does when sucky things strike? Can you see how the more you support yourself and choose self-talk that is supportive and empowering, the less trauma and heartache you create for yourself?

It's not always easy, but the more you practice it, the better you get at it. The great thing about it is that even if you've processed something badly the first time, you can always go back and change the way you look at it. Even years afterwards, you can make changes to how you deal with or process things.

Ask yourself the following questions:

(Or simply fill in the worksheet in your resource kit at: www.tayamicola.com/resourcekit)

- What are some events that have led to your life feeling sucky for you now?
- How have you processed them?
- Have you processed them at all?
- When you reflect on those events, what are the main thoughts that still come up when you talk to yourself about them?
- Are they negative, unsupportive, or disempowering?
- What can you change so that your way of processing the events is still true, but more supportive for you?

Remember, you don't want to just survive, you want to thrive, so supporting yourself with the right self-talk is a skill worth mastering. It's also not as hard as you think.

I want you to really embrace this new way of thinking. It will help you so much, and you really deserve to heal and have a life that doesn't suck. We are quite thorough about this in clinic. It can be much easier with another person to help you, but another way to do this on your own is through journaling.

Journaling is powerful and will help you, but only if you use it.

Journaling is one of the most underrated tools to help one's self. I was originally very resistant to journaling. Probably because I'm such a thinker and an analyzer by nature, I thought journaling wasn't for me. When I first mention it, about two-thirds of my clients are, as well. This is because we think it is something it's not.

Hard.

When I say journal, I don't mean writing long novellas for two hours every day. I don't mean the kind the ship's captain keeps, either. You don't need to write very much or even for very long to get a healing effect. Journaling is simply getting some of your thoughts down on paper.

One of the reasons it is so effective is because we write things we haven't yet thought about. You can have the same thoughts running through your head about your situation day after day, but if you journal about it, new insights and understandings are suddenly revealed. This is because we use a completely different part of our brain to *write* our feelings and problems than we do to *think* our feelings and problems.

It also gives you the chance to get those thoughts outside of yourself: a written record of things you can keep if you need, but they're no longer inside of you.

Journaling can also make your problems

simpler. If you need to say what's going on or how you're feeling in words, you'll tend to express it more succinctly because you have to find the words to describe what you're feeling or thinking fully.

Journaling can give you clarity, understanding, and new insights, but most of all it can give you relief.

I recommend 5–10 minutes of journaling.

Set a timer for 10 minutes and just get everything out.

Don't think...Write.

Don't censor yourself or be politically correct. In fact, be as petty and pathetic as you possibly can, because that's the stuff underneath it all that you need to get out. It's also where the gold hides.

Use the worksheet in the resource kit to do this exercise now. Or create a reminder in your calendar and schedule it in, but don't skip it.

66

"I have the following to say about
_____"

I am here with you to support you. You can be here to support you, too. Together we are going to help you through this and you will see that your life WILL turn around.

Mantras can also help you deal with hard stuff. They are a statement or affirmation that helps you find strength when you need it. A mantra also inspires your inner wisdom to come forth.

When my daughter was unwell, she faced many tests and doctors, most with disappointing results. Each time we got some bad news or test results she said the following mantra:

"There are always exceptions to every rule."

If we received a really bad prognosis we said, "There are always, ALWAYS exceptions to every rule." It became our mainstay. It was her anchor in a treacherous sea, supporting her.

My daughter is quite tall for her age. She

has always been in the top 99th percentile for her height, compared to other children her age.
She was the tallest child in her kindergarten class and has generally been the tallest girl in her grade every year of school. She stands at least a head taller than the other tall children her age.

There is nothing wrong with that. There are children in her grade who are in the bottom 99th percentile for their height. There is nothing wrong with that, either.

I am the shortest person in my family and the shortest person I know.
Short genes run strong in my family. My husband is 6 foot tall. Height runs in his family on his father's side. But he is the shortest in his family and takes after his mother, whose family is also short. My eldest daughter runs short for her age too.

From a height perspective, on many accounts, Caterina is simply the exception to the rule.

This is the metaphor we chose to use

whenever we did any work on being the exception.

No matter what the circumstances are, there are always exceptions to the rule. In her case, we badly wanted her health and wellbeing to not suck. We wanted her to have a wonderful, unlimited life, and the only thing standing in her way was this silly pain/disorder thing. So we focused all our efforts on her being the exception to the rule. When the doctors told her what she could expect down the road, she would say in her mind, "But there are always exceptions to the rule. I am already the exception to the rule with my height, I am used to being the exception to the rule, so this is no different." Her brain responded beautifully.

What mantras can you choose to help you and support you?

Remember, what you tell yourself has power. Spend some time reflecting and choose a mantra to support you. Let your inner wisdom choose or create one for you that resonates deeply.

The great thing about mantras is that they're often created by people who are connected to their inner wisdom so they help us at that very deep level.

Your mantra can be your strength in your stormy sea. It can shelter and protect you more than you may realize.

Things have been hard enough for long enough and you deserve that inner shelter and protection. You deserve a life that doesn't suck.

You will see in the resource kit that there is a whole section on how to create a mantra that suits you and your situation, or you can choose from some of the best I've compiled for you.

Go get your mantra!

In the next chapter, we'll be looking at letting go of things you cannot control.

Your self-talk
has to support
and EMPOWER
you in your
situation.
Anything else
creates baggage
and makes it
harder to
get over.

Chapter 5
Let Go Of Things You Cannot Control

There are always going to be things we cannot control, and some things we put up with that we don't need to. In this chapter, we'll dive deep into tidying up what you can and can't control.

Ok, let's reassess things.

How many things that make your life suck are things that you don't *really* need to put up with?

This is a tricky question.

Life kind of has this way of making us feel like we just have to accept things. Like when you're told or you tell yourself, "There's nothing I can do. This is the way

things are. Deal with it."
When life sucks, you might need to ask yourself if you need to quit what is toxic in your life:

Boss
Marriage
Relationship
Friend
Family
Living Environment
Job
Mortgage
Expenses

One of my girlfriends (let's call her Sunny) recently went through a situation where she was quite severely bullied at work. At first, Sunny thought she was imagining things and felt as if maybe she was being a bit paranoid. Could this really be happening? As events escalated, it just became clearer and clearer (and suckier and suckier) for Sunny that her boss was emotionally abusing her.

Being the self-aware and beautiful soul that she is, Sunny tried intervention, mediation, and all sorts of things to put things right, but even though we have strong anti-bullying awareness in Australia, she basically wasn't supported within her organization. This went on for months...

Her bullying boss then started going through some messy personal issues with her husband, and guess who bore the brunt of her highs and lows? Yep, you guessed it...Sunny.

Sunny rang me one day asking for some support, as she was really struggling to stay strong and hang in there.

I reminded her: "You don't actually need this job."

Sunny replied, "But I love this about it...and I love that about it...and it pays well...and I can't afford not to work..."

I gently reminded her, "You can get another job that pays well and be happy in that one too, hon."

Sunny sent me a text the very next morning, telling me she had applied for a temporary job in another area within the same organization and she'd gotten it. Within 24 hours her life didn't suck. A few weeks later we caught up, and she blissfully announced how very different everything was now that she had removed herself from that toxic situation.

I know that by honoring her worth and both continuing to listen to her inner wisdom and supporting herself with positive self-talk, Sunny's temp role will lead her down a new pathway that's absolutely wonderful.

I want you to be on a wonderful pathway too.

So, let's think carefully...

Is the reason your life sucks because you're putting up with something you don't need to?

It's a great question that your inner wisdom can help you answer. Often we feel we have to put up with things we really don't.

You have more control than you realize. Use it.

So what about the things you cannot control?

Sigh...there are a few of those, aren't there?

You cannot control:

The weather
Natural disasters
Traffic
The financial economy
Physical things (and whether they break down or not)

Even harder, you cannot control:

What others think (including what they think of you)
What others do
What others say
How others behave

How others feel
How others respond
or even what life choices they make.

We also can't control what has happened
in the past or what's going to happen in
the future.

Please, please, please learn to accept these
things. Acceptance is a powerful ally.

*"God grant me the serenity to accept the
things I cannot change, courage to change
the things I can, and the wisdom to know
the difference"*

Worrying about or fighting with the things
you cannot control will quickly create a life
for you that sucks.

Byron Katie wrote a whole book on this
called *Loving What Is*. In it, she famously
says, "When you fight with reality you
lose, but only 100% of the time."

You can't fight with reality and win. That
is like crying because the sky is blue but
you think in order to be happy you need it

to be green. You have no control over what color the sky is, and fighting with that is useless.

So is fighting with your partner because they don't think the same way you do. If they don't already, they're never going to.

Fighting with or about things you can't control is useless and makes you miserable. You can't control that stuff. What you CAN control are your thoughts and your feelings.

Stay with me a moment...

I want you to think about what makes you UN-happy in your life...

Hold that thought for a moment....

I bet you begin to feel something. Maybe a few things.

As you hold onto those feelings, what other thoughts pop into your mind?

Hold on to those for a second...

These thoughts will create more feelings or intensify the ones that are already there. Our thoughts and feelings are inextricably linked.

But guess what? You control your thoughts. 100% of them.

Instead of letting your thoughts run wayward and have all the power in your mind, you need to take back command of them. By doing this, you will also be freeing yourself of the many emotions you are torturing yourself with.

Remember, you are the sovereignty of your own mind. You are in charge. You decide what you think. It's your mind.

It's also a beautiful mind with lots to offer the world. Your mind and your special way of thinking is a gift to us all. When you use it to help others and the world, great things happen.

You make our day better, just by being you and thinking in that very special way that you do. Don't be bashful; it's true and you know it.   When you're doing those things you do to make other people's lives better, our lives don't suck — all because of you.

It's one of my all-time favorite things about you!

I look forward to when you use that beautiful mind of yours to help you more often (much more often, please) in the same way you help us.

And all of this begins with you letting go of worrying about or trying to control the things you can't control.

The sky is not green.

It will never be green, and if it could be green it would not be because of any of the things you are doing.

Got it? Good.

In the next chapter, we'll be helping your mind adjust and prepare for change.

Worrying about
or fighting with
the things you
cannot control
will quickly
create a life
for you that
sucks.

Chapter 6
What's Happening Now Isn't Forever

I know what's happening sucks, but here is another beautiful truth. Whether it's something from your past that's messing up your now, or whether its something you are currently going through, it cannot last forever. Every drought that has ever afflicted the earth has broken at some point.

You see, everything has a beginning and an end.

Just as there was a point or a moment when everything began, there will be a point or a moment where it ends. Sometimes we need to remind our brain about this truth.

I will never forget the day my GP told my daughter and I that her pain would be forever. My mantra at the time was, "This too shall pass."

Even though we were facing (at that time) a forever diagnosis, I knew that our circumstances would change even if her pain didn't.

We were already gathering help, tools and resources. I knew we would deal with it and get better at managing it, and the hell we were living in would change because change is inevitable and those of us who are open to it find it more readily.

Another great mantra I use a lot in clinic is, "There is a way." There is always a way to change what is happening in ways that serve everyone involved.

We can call on our angels and the Universe to help us find these ways. We ask for help in our thinking when we cannot see HOW things CAN turn out. We can use positivity to help us be open to receiving what we need.

But you need to get behind yourself about it in order to see it, and I know sometimes that can be hard.

I have a client with an autistic son. He is four years old. To say my client was unhappy and traumatized would be an understatement. In a moment of exasperation, she cried out, "This is my life, it will NEVER change."

I said: "So this... what you're going through today is exactly what you'll be dealing with when he's 24? I guarantee you'll have a different life when he's 24. Your day won't look like this."

We laughed about the fact that he might still have trouble keeping his shoes on, but life would be different. We then made a list of all the possible changes that could happen in that time.

- The two of them could receive more assistance.
- The government could fund research with groundbreaking information.
- Technology could invent many things that could make life easier or even possible for him to manage more on his own.
- There could be new treatment.
- There could be new legislation and services that make society more supportive, like a seat on the bus with a soundproof booth for autistic travelers, or free massage services for their caregivers. (Can you see how much fun we had with this?)
- They could meet wonderful new friends or people who would offer their support.
- He could improve his function naturally with time.

At this point she joked that he could even fall in love with a caregiver and get married and move out, and then she had to admit she would miss him terribly.

You never know what is going to happen and we often can't control things, but you can bet that change can and will happen.

The people who benefit most from change are the ones who are open to it and ready to act when it arrives. They are the people who whisper supportive mantras to themselves at night like: "What's happening now isn't forever," and "There is a way."

Plan for your circumstances to change.

Engage your inner wisdom. That deeper part of you, your *true self,* isn't damaged. It is NOT wounded, divorced, bankrupt, separated, financially destitute, abandoned or betrayed. Those are just things that have happened. They affect you, but they are not *who* you are deep inside.

Your deeper, wiser self is still ok. Bring them out and let them help you find your way towards an amazing life.

If you can't put an end to your sucky

circumstances just yet, put an end to letting it affect you. How you feel now won't be how you feel forever... unless you want it to be.

Put an end to the things you can control OR put an end to the trauma you feel because of things you can't control.

Let the trauma be over when you leave the relationship, and then let the separation process be simply logistics. No matter what the other person does to try and reengage you, you can still powerfully decide to put an end to its effect on you.

But, do you know what?

Even if you do absolutely nothing, what you're going through now will surely end.

It has to. It must.

Take comfort in knowing that the things that are happening to you now will be different in the future.

In the next chapters, we'll cover:

- The mindset you need to support yourself with whilst you await change.
- What to do to shift your thinking when you're living in the past, and even:
- How and why we feel intense feelings.

Stick with me through these chapters and you'll come out not only feeling so much more aware but things will also begin to make more sense.

There is always
a way to change
what is happening
in ways that
serve everyone
involved.

Chapter 7
Focus On The Outcome

When life sucks we tend to spend so much time in the past, but we need to keep looking forward if we ever want to create some positive changes.

"But I can't stop thinking about what sucks all the time!!!"

That is your brain doing everything it can to problem-solve it. This is usually a sign that you may not have processed it properly. Some people need more help with this so in this chapter we'll be looking at moving forward rather than staying focused on all the toughness about your situation.

In my clinic I help clients identify what's driving the constant desire to play the tape or broken record again. It's usually a fear that you have deep down about what has happened. Once this is addressed, the tape stops playing.

It is important to stay focused on solutions. Whenever you find yourself thinking about it, stop and think about how you would rather things were: that moment when it's all over and your situation has been resolved. If you stay positive and focused on the outcome you want, your brain does this wonderful trick of closing the gap for you. It secretly searches for opportunities for the outcome to come true.

Don't forget to use your inner wisdom. Not to analyze the problem, but to help you find the solution.

Ask the Universe to help, also. They have contacts and resources you don't. It's great to have friends in high places, and you could use a little of this magic in your life now.

There's something else even more wonderful you can do to help with this, and it's something I would LOVE for you to do, anyway.

Plan some nice things.

Make plans to do wonderful things. Plan a getaway, a holiday, or a picnic. Plan big things and small things. It's more valuable that you plan lots of nice little things than one big outlandish thing. (Unless, of course, you have the budget; then go right ahead and do both.) But just plan some nice things.

Give yourself some things to look forward to... In fact, do as much as your circumstances will allow.

When my daughter was unwell, we planned to have a picnic across the road in the park. When we were in the hospital we planned morning tea in the sun on a verandah in the ward next door, or we would plan for her favorite meal to be brought in for dinner.

They were tiny things at first but we planned them and they made SUCH a difference. On the day of her MRI we set a goal to be able to eat high tea at her favorite café as soon as she was well enough. It gave her something to work towards and gave us both something to look forward to. Each time we got to do our special things we soaked it in and used it as fuel to keep going. Any time things got difficult, we would spend some time thinking about our end goal and the next special thing we had planned.

Because of all the nice plans we made and things we did, we suddenly had lots to be grateful for, as well as things to distract ourselves with and to look forward to when those hard times and sucky thoughts crept in.

Of course, we let ourselves be sad from time to time, but we also let ourselves have reasons to be happy, and we used those reasons in as many ways as we could.

After she was declared in remission, she went on a lovely holiday with her sister to her grandparents' property. She continues to plan nice things, and so should you.

Go on…treat yourself. Lets make it simple and plan to spend the next chapter of this book doing something nice together, just you and me.

You could run a lovely bath and read a bit in there while you soak away your stress. You could take me to your favorite coffeehouse and read with me there. Come on — plan some non-sucky time right now and give yourself some things to look forward to.

The next chapter is going to be a chapter that brings a lot of relief as we look at why things feel worse, and how to make them feel ok again.

I'll put the kettle on, and you put the kettle on, and we'll have a cup of tea together.

(Pauses for kettle to boil)

Now sip slowly...

Ahhh...bliss.

**Make plans
to do
wonderful
things...**

Chapter 8
Understanding How Your Past Is Still Affecting You

In this chapter, while we drink tea together—or however you've decided to soak away your tension—we're going to be looking at your files. You should probably know something about them.

Files?

Yes, the ones you keep stored away inside yourself.

Everything that's ever happened, everything you've ever heard, learned, experienced and lived, is in there. If there's one thing I do every single day when I'm working with people, it's reorganize, empty, or replace emotional and mental files.

Think of it like this: Your brain is like a computer. When you experience an emotion, it will open up a file and store that emotion in that file somewhere in your body or your energy field for safekeeping.

You could be five years old and experience 'helplessness' for the first time. Maybe it's a really BIG stress, so you feel it really powerfully. Let's give it a number and measure that you experience helplessness at 80%. Your brain files and tucks that away.

The next time you experience that specific form of helplessness could be weeks, months, or even many years later. Let's say you experience it again at 17 years of age. This time it only measures in as a 10% stress. Your brain will take that 10% and add it into the file with the 80% you felt when you were five. You then experience the event as a combined feeling of 90%.

Later on in life you may feel 'helplessness'

again, but the next time you feel this it might be 2% or 5%. Instead of feeling helplessness at these lower percentages, you experience feelings of helplessness at a combined level of 92 or 95%, completely out of proportion to the current event you are actually dealing with.

This is when we start to say to ourselves:

"I don't understand...."
"This isn't a very big deal..."
"I've been through way worse than this before, but I just can't seem to get on top of things..."

When our files get really full like this, it can feel as if we're falling apart.   We grapple with the weight of our feelings without understanding why they are so strong and what is causing them. It can start to feel as if you're going crazy in your age, or that there is something wrong with you.

If you don't realize what is happening, reflecting on your past struggles only confuses this more because the emotions you felt back then don't match what you are feeling now.

I first learned this file analogy from Phillip Rafferty, the founder of Kinergetics (a style of Kinesiology), and it profoundly changed my treatment plan with clients.

Once we find the underlying emotions associated with the trauma and reduce the percentages of stress, my clients can quickly get on top of their current problems. We can't make it so those past memories are erased or feel as though the events that caused them never happened, but we can quickly and easily reduce how much stress is unconsciously carried in the body.

Just having an understanding of how files work makes a huge impact on their recovery, and clients often feel as if a weight has been lifted off them.

You now have this understanding, too, and so this is something I really want you to grab ahold of. You don't have to be

AFRAID of your intense feelings.

One of the reasons you could be feeling them so strongly is because you've been through so much already. Be compassionate with yourself about it. Use your positive self-talk and your inner wisdom. Remember what we said in chapter 5?

Your *true* self isn't wounded, damaged, or helpless.

These emotions can give you clues about what you need to let go of from your past, and what you need to process better.

Never be afraid or hesitant to enlist professional help with this. Your mental health is worth protecting.

In the next chapter, we'll explore how to stop repeating the same old patterns over and over. It's time to take a look at making some awesome changes, so turn the page and lets get cracking.

**Your true
self isn't
wounded,
damaged
or helpless.**

Chapter 9
Is There A Pattern To Your Tough Times?

In this chapter, we'll look at if what you're going through isn't just another part of a pattern for you.

Sometimes what we are experiencing is stuff we've experienced before. The same hurt and pain, different story. Know what I mean?

While we weave the coincidences together, you can choose to see things in one of these ways:

You can conclude that these are life lessons sent to you to deal with.

You could ascertain that they are things you keep attracting.
Or at the very least, you can simply recognize that you're processing things in a way that continuously creates situations that make your life suck.

What do I think?

I believe some things are sent to us to deal with. I believe luck exists and, unfortunately, sometimes it's bad. But I also know for a fact that I have patterns, and you do too.

Our brains love patterns. Patterns to your brain are like templates, inner frameworks that we can operate from. You may not be great at recognizing patterns in your life, but I bet you are great at recognizing them in others. It's often that way...

We see in our friends how time and time again they get themselves into a situation they've already been in.

You do it, too, you know...But you are less inclined to notice the part you play in your problems. You aren't the reason your life sucks, but you are absolutely the one who has all the power to fix it.

Remember, *you* control you, so that means you control your patterns too. Use that amazing inner wisdom to help you with this. Start seeing what you need to see to turn your life around.

Because of those files, we tend to feel our emotions more intensely when we are in a pattern cycle. If you notice your emotions rising, there could be a pattern looming.

Right before we start saying, "Here we go again," know that it is okay. You are still lovable. I haven't left you yet, and you haven't left you yet, so let's dig deeper and learn.

When you think about what sucks in your life, are there some patterns behind it?
Have you been here before?
Do you have a pattern of:

- Giving up halfway through?
- Dating the same person?
- Sabotaging your chances at love?
- Making your happiness dependent on other things or people?
- Never having enough money?

Let's see if we can help with that right now. Go grab a piece of paper and a pencil, (or simply fill out the pattern worksheet in your resource kit).

Pick something sucky that's happened or is happening for you now...

Write down the important factors about that situation. What do you not like about it? What is significantly sucky about it? What emotions do you feel?

When you look at the factors, has this ever happened to you before?

Sometimes it's as plain and simple as picking all the times you had a break-up. Sometimes it's not that obvious.

What if what's happening has never happened before?

Have the factors contributing to what you're currently going through happened before?

There is an example of this in the following table on the next page.

Sucky thing = I've injured my back and I'm not able to work.

Factors: I feel powerless and weak. I can't control what's happening; I wish I could just get better, but I can't. I need to rely on other people, which I hate. The friends I thought I had aren't here for me like I thought they would be.

Q: Has this happened before?
A: No, I've never had a bad back. I've never been away from work for more than a week.

To explore this further and find the pattern, we need to look deeper at the significant factors.

Q's:
Have you ever felt powerless and weak?
Have you ever had to rely on others?
Have people you thought were friends ever really abandoned you?
A: Yes — When my marriage fell apart, I felt really powerless. I ended up moving back in with my parents and I hated it. There were also two friends I thought I could lean on, but they sided with my ex.
From this scenario, we can deduce that there may be a pattern of choosing unsupportive friends.

Get the picture?

If you can't think of times when the exact thing has happened before, check the significant factors. Often times, they are there if we look at the problem in a unique way and if we're willing to dig deep enough.

Lets get back to you and your stuff, making sure you call on your inner wisdom to help you with this (and remembering your inner wisdom doesn't just babble stuff out, so you'll need to be patient).

So you've got something that's not great now, something that's making your life suck. And you've got your significant factors.

Pick another time when you went through something similar. Write down the significant factors from that event.

- What is the same about the two of them?

- What was different about these two times?
- What was different about YOU?
- What have you learned about yourself?
- Instead of just noticing what is wrong, notice what is right.
- What learnings and lessons do you need to apply from this discovery to help you with what's happening now?

Stay in this self-reflective space while you wait for your answers to bubble up....

If you've identified any patterns, what is a more empowering way to think and behave?

Don't worry if you find this process difficult. It can be. Sometimes you need someone else to help you connect the dots and to help you get to the root of the problem. You really just need to look for similarities and differences. I'd love to help you with this, but perhaps a trusted friend can help you?

Looking at your patterns and calling on your inner wisdom allows your soul to grow and expand. Your wisdom gets even wiser, and you free yourself from the need to repeat the same patterns in life. In fact, just connecting the dots tends to free you.

Yay...go you!

You just grew a little more.

"In life you will realize there is a role for everyone you meet. Some will test you, some will use you, some will love you, and some will teach you. But the ones who are truly important are the ones who bring out the best in you. They are the rare and amazing people who remind you why it's worth it." — Unknown

In the next chapter, we'll take a look at where you are on your recovery roadmap. Knowing where you are helps you navigate through and forward more quickly. Turn the page to get started.

In life you will
realise there is
a role for everyone
you meet.
Some will test you,
some will use you,
some will love you
and some will teach you.
But the ones who
are truly important
are the ones who
bring out the best in you.
They are the rare and
amazing
people who remind
you why it's worth it.
- Unknown.

Chapter 10
What Stage Are You In?

In this chapter we're going to help you identify where you are at with everything, and help you quickly move through to the other side.

You were born with an amazing healing mechanism inside of you. Your self-repair system gets to work whenever you get hurt. If you get a paper cut, every cell in your body knows its job and begins to repair that cut for you immediately. Within a week you have no evidence, or little evidence, it even happened. If you didn't understand this process when you first started to bleed, you might be very concerned at your body's reaction and think things were never going to be the same again. We trust our bodies to heal our cuts and bruises and we leave them to get on with it.

You have that same mechanism in place to deal with tough times. Just like healing a cut, there are certain stages you will instinctively go through that help your mind heal and process what's happening. Understanding a bit more about these stages can help you move through them more easily so you can process the tough times in better ways.

Every experience is unique, and every person's reaction to tough times is equally unique, so you may or may not experience all the stages when dealing with your situation. Although there is a general order, you may experience the stages out of order, or even skip a stage entirely.

There are advantages and disadvantages to each stage. If you know these advantages, you can put them to good use. If you know the disadvantages, you can hopefully avoid the pitfalls and not get stuck in them for too long.

It's also critical to note that while many experts have created different models of the stages you may go through, I've listed the main ones I see repeatedly with my clients in my clinic. These are some of the ones famously coined by Elizabeth Kübler-Ross in her book *On Death and Dying,* published in 1969.

See if you can identify yourself in any of these stages. Are you making good use of them?

Denial

Refusal to accept what is happening. "I can't believe it."

This stage is one we all usually pass through quite quickly. The healing advantages of this stage give you the chance to catch your breath and slowly process the shock of what has happened or is happening. It also gives you the chance to momentarily keep your life in order. Denial allows you to ease into what is happening at a pace you can handle more easily. The obvious disadvantages of this stage are that as long as you remain in this stage, healing cannot take place on any level. Choosing to ignore something usually just makes the problem get bigger.

Anger/Blame
"If _____ didn't happen, none of this would have happened. Why me?"

Anger gets a really bad rap from society thanks to all the damage it can do when it is not safely expressed or used for healthy purposes.
The advantages of anger are that it is very fuelling. Anger ignites a spark in us to help thrust us forward, moving us out from where we are (a hurtful or unhealthy place) into a place we would rather be. It attacks the threats that stand in our way, and encourages us to fight back against them.

"I can't take this any longer," or "No, this can't be happening," etc.

It's an adaptive reaction to threat that appears around tough times when someone or something is threatening our happiness. In my experience, it's because we want things to be different to how they are, and anger can give you the energy to deal with that.

It can provide you with the go-forward you need. You can use anger to propel you towards acceptance or toward making courageous decisions. It can help you find your strength to fight back and claim your happiness.

It's ok to be angry, especially when difficult situations have happened. It's not ok to destroy others' happiness in the process. It's NOT OK to let it rip. You need to find ways to release it safely and constructively. Similarly, unexpressed anger can cause just as much hurt. We can become passive aggressive and destructive in other ways as a result.

The message is obvious. Don't bottle anger. Don't let it eat away at you or destroy your life and those around you. Instead, recognize that it is normal, and find ways to *SAFELY* express and release it.

Grief/Depression
"What's the point?"

Grief is often an overlooked part during any tough times. We don't necessarily have to lose someone significant to be in this stage. We can suffer losses in many ways.

Think about when a relationship ends. Here are some losses that may arise as a result: Loss of love, loss of a future together, loss of lifestyle, loss of support, loss of role, loss of income, loss of self-esteem, etc.

And when suffering health issues: Loss of independence, loss of vitality, loss of abilities, loss of hope, loss of earning power, loss of appearance, loss of productivity, loss of meaning, loss of identity, loss of function, loss of having your own life, loss of the future.

No matter what you are experiencing, there will be losses of some kind. You can see how certain events can create grief on many levels.
Although grief and sorrow are not afflictions we would wish on anyone, this stage can actually be useful in moving you

closer to acceptance.   Grief and sorrow can create a desire to hibernate and close off from the larger view of life. This retreating can create a recuperative space for reflection. While in this stage, your ability to access your deeper, wiser inner mind is easier than in any other stage.

The drawback of this phase is that you can feel helpless or that the situation is hopeless, when in reality you never are, and it rarely is.

Remember... There is always a way...

Another more serious drawback from this stage is that it can lead to depression. While some degree of depression in sucky circumstances is normal and to be expected, if you feel at any point it's getting the best of you, reach out immediately. Tough times are one thing, but having them affect your mental health is quite another.

Acceptance
"What's done is done"

Acceptance brings with it finality. When you can accept that it happened, you can begin to embrace and build peace again within yourself. We cannot put anything behind us until we fully accept that things have occurred. Once you acknowledge the reality of your circumstances, you can begin to move on. Though acceptance is the shining light to reaching the other side of tough times, it has its difficulties too.

It can be hard to admit things sometimes.

Where do you fit in these stages? Can you relate to any when you think about your tough times? How can you make use of the stages as a resource instead of viewing it as an arduous journey?

Your self-compassion and self-support are monumental allies for helping you move through these stages and into a place of recovery. Be gentle with yourself when you experience the difficulties that can arise from them, but look for the strengths they will give you too.

They are part of your self-repair system.

Don't fight them...embrace them. In doing so, you are allowing those cuts and bruises to heal.

In the next chapter, we will be looking at making sure we move through things instead of creating baggage.

Are you ready?

We cannot
put anything
behind us until
we fully accept
that things
have occurred.

Chapter 11
The Top Emotions That Cause Baggage

In this chapter, we'll learn how to deal with baggage. We'll deal with guilt, grief, abandonment, trust, and fear.

Let's begin.

Although there are a myriad of emotions we can feel when experiencing tough times, there are a handful of them that time and time again are responsible for creating emotional baggage.

More than anything, I want you to let go of the things that create baggage, and that means helping you process them better so hopefully you can create a life that doesn't suck.

If you hold onto them, or process them poorly, baggage is bound to result... Yuck!

So these are the top emotions I repeatedly come across that create baggage.

Guilt
Yup — has to be number 1.

What is guilt even for? Well, I'll tell you. It is closely tied to that internal compass of ours that lets us know when we've done something wrong.

It could be a mistake that we've made, or perhaps a poor decision. It also occurs when we think we've upset someone else's moral compass. Guilt results when we hold ourselves to our own highest standard or someone else's highest standard.

That means:

1. You did or have done something that you wish you hadn't done. For whatever reason, you made a mistake, or a bad decision. Now you feel guilty.

Or

2. You did, or have done something that you think someone else wishes you hadn't done.

Guilt alerts us to the conflict inside of ourselves that we have.

Guilt is surprisingly easy to conquer in 3 steps.

If you feel guilty because of something you did or didn't do:

1st Step: Don't do it again. Simple.
2nd Step: Apologize, sincere and from the heart. ONCE.
3rd Step: Make it right. Usually, this is simply done by step number two. If however, you have a gap to fill — fill it.

Done.

You cannot turn back time. You cannot undo what you did. You cannot make them get over it or heal. What's done is done. Continuing to feel bad will not help with any of these things, either.

If you are truly sorry, a good friend will understand. If they don't, there is nothing you can do. No matter how much you beat yourself up about it, it will not and cannot change those things. If someone continues to make you feel bad, then I would seriously question your friendship.

Thing is, I need to put a paragraph in here just in case you're one of those people who feel guilt for absolutely no reason. You haven't done anything wrong, no one else thinks you have, either, but you've decided to feel guilty about little nothings, anyway.

Can I please make something very clear?

The fact that you even register guilt means you are a good person. You care. People who don't care don't have that moral compass. This means you get to relax more than most people. Very caring people aren't hurtful or wrong. A person who cares that much does not need to self-check every tiny situation, every exchange made, or every instance to make sure they haven't offended or that others are ok. It's not in your nature to offend, so you won't.

Once my clients fully understand that if they are one of those people who *really* care about others, they never have to self-check. Life changes in magical ways for them.

Accept your imperfections. No one is going to get everything right all the time. Perfection is not attainable. You are perfect within your limitations. When you compare yourself to others or feel guilty about your imperfections, you are expecting yourself to be faultless. Accept your faults and move on.

You don't need to carry this guilt around any longer. It won't help you, and it wont help anyone else.

Here is the number one thing you need to know about guilt.... Are you ready?

Actions change things, not guilty feelings.

Act on the things you are unhappy about and let the guilt go.

Grief

At the time of writing this chapter, I am working through quite a bit of grief. My nanna passed away only three weeks ago. We were very close.

I am still raw with the tragedy of it. I couldn't even open my laptop to write this chapter until now. I've written around it. In the short space of time it has taken me to face this chapter, I can already begin to see how I've moved through Denial, Anger, and Depression. I've even done a bit of bargaining (if you bring her back, I'll never...etc.).

For the first few days, I knew she was gone but couldn't quite believe all the 'nevers' I suddenly had about her: All the things that could never happen because she was no longer here.

It will be quite some time, I think, before I can accept that she has gone. Logically, I know she will never truly be gone, and logically I know that I said everything I needed to say, that we will have each other in spirit, and that we will still 'talk' every day. And logically I understand that at 85 she lived a great life and I can't expect her to live forever.

But grief is not logical.

My heart is heavy, and will be for quite a while.

The first step is to be gentle with you, especially when others are not. Society is really good at letting us know we can't rush grief, but then it does the exact opposite and expects us to be over it quickly. People will tell you to take your time and that what you're going through is HUGE. They'll even admit they couldn't possibly understand what you're going through, but in a month's time, they'll wonder why you're still not back to normal.

They may even tell you that they're here for you anytime, but then you'll realize after a few phone calls that when you ring, they quickly change the subject. Well-meaning, caring, beautiful folks are guilty of this. We all are.

Work will tell you initially, "Take as much time as you need," but then stop paying you after two weeks have passed.

You'll do it to yourself too. You'll chastise yourself about how long it is taking you. You'll be impatient with your own recovery.

All of this is normal.

Be ok with it.

It can take many, many years (not weeks) to adjust when a significant person in your life passes. That's not to say you are going to feel this low and horrible for years. But we heal incrementally. So, you will come a little forward and you may go a little back, but you will heal at the rate you heal, not at the rate everyone else has in mind for you.

As I discussed in the last chapter, we can experience loss from many things. One of the ways we can move forward from loss and grief is to hold on to the elements or things that can never be taken away.

As I was very close to my grandmother, there are a lot of things I can hold on to that time, circumstances, and death can never take away.

If you are grieving someone or something very dear to you, you will have received something in return just for having them (or it) in your life. What will you always have because of them? What will stand the test of time, no matter what?

My grandmother is the reason I am so spiritually connected. She passed on a set of very special gifts that have enhanced my life and the lives of others. While I was born with these extra sensitivities, it wasn't until my teens that I realized where they came from.

She was the person who taught me to meditate and to commune with my higher self and inner wisdom. Nothing and no one can take these things away from me. These things cannot be lost. I will have them forever.

Realizing and acknowledging what will remain and what can never be taken away can transcend grief and give you the peace you deserve throughout this process.

I want you to be gentle with yourself about it. Whether it happened 20 years ago, or 20 months ago or two weeks ago, it's ok if you are still sad.

Did you hear me? It is ok...

It is ok if you still want to cry because of it.

When you remember them, think of what you will always have and what cannot be taken away.

It will help, I promise.

Abandonment

Abandonment is intricate in its complexities. On one level, abandonment contains grief and loss. On another level, it forces the person to question their worth and address feelings of rejection, and on another it creates trust issues. Exploring feelings of abandonment can be like navigating a minefield.

There is one thing that transcends abandonment every time. There is one person who will never abandon you, and that is *you*.

If you can build a relationship with yourself that you can depend on, then depending on others is suddenly not so risky, and if someone pulls the rug from under you, you aren't so left out in the cold.
You can begin to put your life back together and even find ways to enjoy life again because you begin to have a stability that cannot be taken away.

Be there for you, knowing that you will never leave you. Be the support to yourself that you are to your closest friends and family. Be there to help yourself, to nurture you and to console you. It sounds crazy, but you would pull out all the stops to support your nearest and dearest.

Using this same mental attitude to help yourself will help you develop that self-trust and self-dependence we look to receive from others.

If some charlatan has left you high and dry, don't abandon yourself at the same time.

You are not empty; you are full.

You are not incapable; you're just hurting and that is ok. But your deeper self is not broken. It has all you need and more to help you get through this. Forgetting that is like letting that charlatan steal from you, then packing them a little bag of extras to help them on their journey.

You are still here.
And the sun keeps rising...
And the days keep coming...
And you deserve to live a not-sucky life.

If you have your own back and a strong sense of trust internally, you will be stronger and more able to choose trustworthy people to spend your time with.

Which leads us to...

Trust
 Many of my clients swing from one extreme to the other around trust. They start out trusting blindly and then when they get hurt, they shut that sucker down and never trust anyone ever again.

There is some middle ground though, isn't there?

Don't trust blindly...trust incrementally. Give people the chance to earn your trust and assess accordingly.

You can benefit from relaxing around

trust. You can benefit from not trusting blindly. Stick to that middle ground and your trust issues become more harmonious.

And don't forget to trust *you*. As we covered in abandonment, building self-trust will give you an unshakable foundation. You are the only one who will ever truly have your back 100%. So if your intuition tells you to be careful of a person and you ignore it, then you are not trusting you.

This comes up again and again when I work with clients. Someone comes into their life and makes a mess of their world and manages to destroy their happiness in the process. But *so often* people tell me they had a hunch about that person when they first met. If they had only trusted themselves and their intuition in the beginning, they could have saved themselves all that heartache.

I encourage you to trust your beautiful inner, wiser self, as it will never lead you astray. You have more answers in you than you realize. You have your own best interests at heart. You are amazing and worthy of your trust, and if you make decisions and listen to the guidance your inner wisdom can provide, you will line up with people who are aligned to your heart space, your needs, and your way of thinking. Equally, you will enrich their lives on the same level.

That is why we come to this planet, to make those beautiful connections. You can make more of these healthy, beautiful connections.

Think about how this book came to you. We found our way to each other. Be open to more good people coming your way. Surround yourself with good people and the hard stuff won't be so hard.

Anger
We touched on this in the last chapter as a phase.

Anger can create baggage for us when it is unresolved or unexpressed, because it builds. When you bottle your anger, it's a bit like a snowball rolling down a mountain. It doesn't look like much to worry about at first until it suddenly gets larger with momentum and wreaks havoc.

The best time to explore your feelings of anger is when you are not angry or triggered in any way. This way you can look at it objectively.

I think the best way to do this is through journaling. Explore your anger with a pen and paper.

Start with: "I am angry because..."

Don't let anything stop you from doing this exercise. Worried about proper grammar? Don't be. Now isn't the time to cross your 't's and dot your 'i's and use your commas. Just journal your feelings — every last one of them. Because, by doing so, you will know exactly what your anger is about. You can then use this information to help you BEFORE you are triggered.

You can choose a safe method to release your anger such as playing racquetball, punching some pillows, or screaming all the things you'd love to say inside your car with the windows rolled up.

This way you get it all out mentally and physically without hurting, harming, or upsetting a single soul.

You can then access your wiser mind to help you find some solutions or make choices that can alleviate your circumstances.

Fear
Fear is the number one feeling that stops us from moving forward.
Fear alerts you to the possibility of danger. It's a survival reflex we need to help us stay alive. The problem is that what we are often afraid of isn't life threatening at all. Even more common is when we fear things knowing there really isn't anything to be afraid of. This is when irrational fear can actually become baggage.

When we feel those strong emotions that

create fear, the part of our brain that controls the fight-or-flight response is activated. The emotion behind the fear might be something completely different — like "I feel embarrassed." If the fight-or-flight reflex was triggered at the same time as you felt the embarrassment or shame, then in the future you may experience fear around potentially embarrassing situations.

Fear can be helpful. It helps us to be prepared. We can use our fear to problem solve potential problems, which is a good thing.

Don't fight your fear: give it a voice to hear its concerns, and then thank it.

We can also reduce our irrational fears with information. The more information you receive about something, the less fearful we become. Fear is triggered partly by the unknown. We don't know how things are going to turn out. We don't know if something is going to be potentially dangerous for us. That's what makes it worse.

It's ok if you're afraid of something. Everyone is. You probably even have great reasons for feeling that fear. Life can be hard, and it makes us question our safety all the time, for good reason.

But if fear is stopping you from having a not-sucky life, then you owe it to yourself to work through it. The easiest way to work through fear is to get more information.

What if you have an irrational fear of starting your own business? Or signing up for online dating?

The more information you get, the less fear you will feel. Do that short course on business before you start. Watch documentaries or read books on what you fear the most about starting one. Eventually, with enough information, the fear will collapse.

If you explore the nature of your fear and release the emotions behind it, there truly will be nothing keeping them in place, and joining that dating website (or whatever you are wanting to do) will be possible and maybe even fun.

You deserve to be released from your fears. You deserve to be filled with positive emotions and excitement about the things you wish to achieve that will make your life meaningful, not sucky. Release yourself from the emotions that disempower you, and embrace the ones that empower you to carve out the life you crave, the life you deserve.

So here is the formula for working through fear:

- Thank your fear for alerting you to possible danger.
- Get as much information as you can to help you move through it.
- Release the emotions that drive or trigger it.

Let's put it into practice.

Grab a piece of paper and answer the following questions:
(Or simply go to the "Fear" exercise in your resource kit).

- What could you do to change your sucky circumstances, but you are too afraid of?
- What ways could you find out more about doing that (eg. books, movies, courses, asking around, internet searching)? And where could you start?
- What emotions are tied to this fear that you need to release?

Following this process will free you from fear and you'll be ready to take on new challenges.

In the next chapter, we are going to help you get over it all.... (Sigh and long exhale).

Turn the page so we can get started.

**Be the support
to yourself
that you are
to your
closest friends
and family.**

Chapter 12
Moving Through It And Building A Bridge.

Finally, we're here!

In this chapter, we're going to learn how to build a bridge and get over our stuff. It's time, don't you think?

We've talked and talked. We've learned (hopefully lots). We've grown...

Let's heal you. Let's get you right past it and through it and out the other side. Let's build your bridge so you can get over it.

Of course, if you're going to get over or through it, you have to release it. Don't hold onto it like it's an old friend — it's not. It's not healthy to be defined by your pain.

Remember, it's how you process things that determine whether you thrive or just merely survive.

Viktor Frankl wrote an amazing book called *Man's Search For Meaning*. As a Holocaust survivor, his beliefs were really tested, but he teaches that we all have an amazing "defiant power of the human spirit." Basically, no matter how bad things are, we always have this ability to tap into our deeper mind and rise above the bad stuff life throws at us. He believed the fundamental difference between pain and suffering was that although pain was a given, suffering is optional. He also thought that suffering or not suffering is how we choose to react to the pain.

Viktor advised that, "Forces beyond your control can take away everything you possess except one thing: your freedom to choose how you will respond to the situation. You cannot control what happens to you in life, but you can always control what you will feel and do about what happens to you."

Basically, no matter how bad our stuff really is, we get to choose how we respond to it. So to process it in a healthy way, you need to change your view of what's happened or happening to one that supports and empowers you.

I want you to think of what it is that you need to get over.

We want to build that bridge and get you to the other side, so if we can pile up all the stuff that you want to get over underneath, then we'll construct away, right over the top of it. Right here, right now.

Get a pencil and paper, (or simply turn to the "Build a Bridge" section in your resource kit). We are going to do this. It's not enough to just read. The magic happens for you when you DO.

I'll put the kettle on again while you do that...

(It's not too soon for another cuppa, is it...? Thank goodness. Pauses until you are ready...)

Write all the benefits that getting over the bad stuff and tough times will give you.

Maybe it's been holding you back and stopping you from doing the things you want to do. Maybe you've noticed you're not as brave or not as trusting because of things that have happened, and you know you probably need to have some trust in order to achieve the things you want to achieve.

Will getting over it allow you to have a loving relationship, a successful career, financial security, deep and meaningful purpose to your life, or true happiness? It could be anything, but because of your stuff those things are suddenly harder to reach.

Maybe you will feel better within yourself, get your self-esteem back, and find your smile again. Maybe you'll have the courage to go back to school, lose the weight, travel, write, get fit, or get your health back on track.

Or maybe you really don't want it to hold you back down the road. Think of your reasons why it will be great to get over it and write them down now.

Start writing anything and everything that comes to mind. Don't censor yourself. Just write. Ramble if you need to—it will help get you going—but write...

Pretty soon, something will take over. You will find yourself getting in 'the zone' and your inner wisdom will get involved and reveal some real gems.

Maybe you'll write a lot, maybe you'll write a little, but just write and get the process started. Think of your reasons for wanting to get over your stuff and all the benefits you'll receive from getting over it.

Finish one or both of the two statements below.

"I want to get over this because…"

or

The benefits of getting over this will be…"

Ok, finished?

These are your powerful reasons to continue. These are what we need your brain to know. We have to sell these to your brain so that it gets on board and helps you. By clearly outlining them, labeling them, and putting them down on paper, you send a powerful message to your mind and your energy that this is worth doing. When you just mull over these things in your mind, analyzing them internally, it's not the same as getting them out of yourself and writing them down.

Writing them down is so much more powerful and revealing, not just to you but to your subconscious mind.

Now that we have your reasons/benefits, flip the page over and write down all the cons. Yep, as crazy as it sounds, write down all your reasons why you *shouldn't* get over it.

Before you say, "There aren't any reasons I shouldn't get over it," think long and hard.

There are always pros and cons to everything. This is where you explore your fears and resistance.

There are always reasons NOT to do something. Maybe getting over it will mean you have to face some fears or do something scary, like change. Maybe these feelings of mistrust protect you from getting hurt. Maybe being more open to finding love will also open you to finding rejection.

This process will reveal different things. If you get a block, just relax, breathe, and invite your inner wisdom to come out.

You might know the answer right away, but often your feelings and wisdom about this will be mostly subconscious, so they'll be coming from a place deep, deep down. That means they can be slower to surface. Be patient, pencil ready...

"I don't want to get over this because..."

"The benefits of not getting over it are..."

Now you have your reasons for resisting it. Well done. You are halfway there.

Both sides of the paper are here to help you. It's wonderful to have these fears and resistance because they are designed to keep you safe. Both sides of the paper want what is best for you. Both sides want you to be a fully functioning and happy human being. Both sides want your life to NOT suck.

This is a good thing.

What can you learn from your fears and resistance? What are they clearly trying to tell you?

Make sure your self-talk is supportive.

The way to move through this is to acknowledge the powerful messages. Your subconscious might not be saying no. It might simply be saying, "Be careful."

How can you move through in a way that serves both sides of the page? Remember that mantra?

"There is a way."

There is always a way that serves every part of you and gives you the best of both worlds.

So if, for example, your issue revolves around trusting others, thank your resistance! Your resistance is right; not everybody deserves your trust.

Make yourself a promise right now that you won't trust others blindly and then get smacked in the face because they suddenly give you a reason not to. When you think about it, that is what most of us do. We trust fully until someone shows us they are not trustworthy, and it's kind of silly. There is a much better way.

From now on, declare:

"I will remember that trust has to be earned. I now lovingly look for evidence in others that they are trustworthy and match my trust in them accordingly."

How empowering is that?

You are now on the lookout for trust, open and ready to meet people, but with a healthy dose of have-you-got-my-back protection? Trust the people who've proven their trust to you.

Win-Win.

See how this works? Have a look at your paper and make amends with both sides of it. As you work through each resistance you are building that beautiful bridge.

Congratulations...I'm so proud of you!

You are amazing! Look how far you have come. Look at what you've achieved. Let's celebrate! Not just with cups of tea, but an actual celebration. Can we go somewhere nice for dinner? Can you cook us up a lovely meal? What IS your favorite meal...? Let's cook it tonight.

Or can we at least share a cuppa AND a biscuit this time?

When do you have time? Can we carve five minutes into your schedule right now?

Let's do this!

THIS milestone is worth celebrating.

You are worth celebrating.

In the next chapter, we'll help you never look back, so turn the page and we can get started.

"I will remember
that trust has
to be earned.
I now lovingly
look for evidence
in others that
they are trustworthy
and match my
trust in them accordingly."

Chapter 13
Don't Be A Victim, Be A Survivor

Now that you're over it, or getting over it, don't look back.

In this chapter, we'll help you do just that.

Guess what? Re-telling your story, playing it over and over in your mind, or holding on to it is looking back. Remember, as much as possible, we want you to thrive.

A victim is someone who has had something wrongful happen to them, and they are harmed or wounded because of it. If you remain a victim, you never really get over it because you are still nursing old hurts.

Staying in this mindset keeps you fearful

and small. It inadvertently feeds your fear without you realizing, and this causes more problems down the road. Your brain starts to keep watch, expecting more bad things to happen to you. It begins to view bad things as your new 'normal' because being a victim is all about YOU. It's personal. It perpetuates a cycle of being chosen for bad things. Hardships can begin to resonate with you. This can affect your energy field, so that you might line up with others who are going through hardships, or perpetuate them. This can affect your mindset, promoting "It's always one thing after another" styles of thinking instead of productive problem solving. It can even affect your subtle body language and the way you communicate unconsciously with others, so you literally put "Pick on me" out there to the world.

A victim is powerless, a pawn who is at the mercy of everything.

A survivor, on the other hand, is someone who has been through something and comes out the other side. They survive it.

Which one sounds better?
Which one is easier?

It can seem harder to let go of the victim and the story, especially if you've been through so very much. However it is actually easier to be the survivor. A victim has to keep dragging it around, reliving and staying in fear, and fear is very draining. A survivor, however, has a beginning and an end to their pain.

I know you're tired.

When you go through tough times, it can feel as though your life force is being sucked out of you. Your mind has to work all day long to solve problems you wish you never had. I'm asking you to dig a little deeper when you might feel like you're already running on reserve power.

I get it...you're drained. But I want you to understand that you have more inside of you than you realize. You were built to survive and make it through. Just when you think you have nothing left, you'll find more.

I watched this happen over and over again with my daughter and her pain levels. She used to say to me, "Mummy, I wish I could give up, but I can't. You think you can't take anymore but you actually have to. You don't get to choose. You think you can't do it, but then you do. I want to give up, but it's impossible."

It was horrible, but powerful at the same time. She would feel so helpless but then feel so surprised and amazed at her own stamina and ability to get through. The first few times it happened was torture. But then she began to feel proud of herself and she began to use her survival mechanism to claw her life back piece by piece and at a steady and growing pace.

Your survival mechanism is strong. Don't fight it...use it.

One day very soon, you will get to the end and realize something about your sucky life.

It *happened.*

See that? *Past* tense. It won't be happening anymore.

When you reach this point, don't hold onto it.

If someone did something to you, don't hold on to that either... but what if it's hard?

In the next chapter, we'll explore what to do if your life sucks because of one person's doing.

A survivor has
a beginning
and an end to
their pain.
Your survival
mechanism is
strong. Don't
fight it... use it!

Chapter 14
Needing Others To Pay

In this chapter, we'll show you how to move on or deal with someone who hurt you.

When our sucky life is largely caused by others, even when we're over it, we can be tempted to harbor a little resentment. Or a lot.

Sometimes it's a lot.

We can feel like we NEED others to get what they deserve, and receive a healthy dose of payback for all the wrongs they've caused us.

Sometimes we can even feel like they got away with it.

It's upsetting because we can feel like there is no retribution for what they've done, but you know what? There is. If a decent person does something wrong, and they don't make it right, it haunts them. (Remember that chapter on guilt??)

Deep down, you know what they did wasn't right — and so do they. No matter how they are pretending to handle it, deep down, they feel ashamed of what they have done, and denying it only makes it worse. They are already paying the price, trust me.

Notice I said, "If they are a decent person."

If the person who caused you so much misery is NOT a decent person, then that is a different story. They won't be able to see a damn thing about where they went wrong, or why it was so bad. They'll either be oblivious, or they may even feel proud of themselves.

Don't be fooled. These people pay a heavy, heavy price too.

People who aren't decent are seriously missing out. Their relationships are shallow and their experience of life is too. This is a truly sad thing. Their life will never have the depth of meaning that true connection to life and others can bring. If they can't feel a connection to other people's pain, then they also can't feel a connection to other people's love. If they lack the ability to feel real empathy towards others, then they can't receive it or provide it properly. This affects all their relationships and experiences profoundly. They are going through life completely missing the point.

These people miss out on the full joy that life can bring and the meaning with which it carries.

You have been through some difficult things, but in time you will put your life back together and find in others what they have been unable to provide.

They will always have something missing.

All you have to do to heal yourself is to remember that the best revenge is living well. Shift your focus from them to you. They are taking up space in your mind. Focus on yourself, not the people who have treated you badly.

Plus, when you truly move on, they will feel it. We all know this and remember it from our earlier dating experiences. When you've loved and shared intimacy with a person, the connection remains for a while. But the moment they see that you're over them and you've moved on — the feeling is cutting. Whatever hold they had on you is no longer there. It's more powerful than anything, and it's all the 'revenge' you will ever need.

I believe just as powerfully that when you truly move on they energetically feel it...even if you never lay eyes on each other again.

Don't wait for the day you spot them in a crowd again. Just get on with your life and enjoy the benefits.

You have so much to offer. Live for you. You are not dead, you are alive and maybe... you're waiting. This is your chance. You can grow or you can stagnate.

In the next chapter, we're going to make you a plan.

Turn the page to begin *your* next chapter.

**Focus on yourself
not the people
who have treated
you badly...**

**You have given
them enough
already.**

Chapter 15
Plan Your Way Out

When life sucks, we need to change things. We need a plan to get out of it. The problems you're dealing with that make your life suck need to change or they need to go.

You can un-suck your life on your own, but I've learned from my clients that those who do well—I mean really, really well— work with a team.

Albert Einstein once said: "You cannot fix a problem with the same thinking that created it."

What other help do you need?

- If you have legal issues, get legal help.
- If you have financial issues, get financial help
- If you have business issues, get business advice
- If you have marriage issues, get marriage help
- If you have work issues, get career help

You get the picture.

Don't surround yourself with sucky people — that's going to make more of your life suck. We need good quality people who are just as dedicated to helping you as you are.

If your budget can't afford an accountant, can you see a student bookkeeper?

If you have work stress or issues, what's already available in your organization? Can you see a career counselor to help you find a job or career more suitable for you? Can you at least take an aptitude test online?

If you need couples counseling to make your life un-suck, but you don't like psychologists or counselors, would you feel more comfortable seeing a pastor or a religious minister who specializes in marriage counseling? Or a relationship coach? Or participate in a yoga retreat for couples?

There are people and professionals who are deeply passionate about helping you, and they have the qualifications, tools, and techniques to help you.

Find them.

Stop thinking there's no way out, or thinking that because you don't know, you can't start. You can!!

If you're strapped for cash, check what is available for free through the government or through non-profit organizations. Ask questions at the doctors. Check with colleges that have supervised clinics (these are amazing as they have everything you need at the right price). Ask neighbors, family, and friends.

Read books on the subject you need help with.

For child abuse, you can't pass up *Healing the Wounded Heart* by Dan B Allender. (I'll warn you, it's not an easy read, but it's incredibly helpful.)

For divorce, try *Crazy Time: Surviving Divorce And Building A New Life* by Abigail Trafford.

For debt and money, try *How To Get Out Of Debt, Stay Out Of Debt & Live Prosperously* by Jerrold Mundis.

Find what and whom you need and give them to yourself.

Ask the Universe for help. Say what you need and then be on the lookout for signs and signals of what direction to go in. Ask the Universe to make the signs REALLY clear.

This will help in three beautiful ways.

1. It will open your spirit up to receiving help from high places.
2. It will open your energy field up to receiving so that more good things can come your way.
3. It will help you to be more open-minded and aware of what is out there, so you mentally start to filter things that don't serve you and draw in what you need to change the suck factor in your life.

(Bonus, bonus, bonus)

Remember, psychological trauma is a pretty big deal. You don't want to make things any worse than they are. If you have some abuse or deep wounds from earlier experiences, please don't mess around. Seek psychological help.

When we get hurt physically, we seek and apply first aid. If, however, you have a gaping wound, you probably need a surgeon.

Don't confuse the two.
When things have been hard for a while
and you've started to move on, it is
common to develop the thinking that the
Universe now owes you something.

Heck, you are probably right. However,
waiting around for something really good
to happen that wipes out all the bad
things could leave you waiting a looooong
time.

I see so many clients do this. My daughter
did it too.

The completely sucky reality is that no
matter how much you've been through
already, life is not like the game of
Monopoly — it won't give you a get-out-of-
jail-free-card.

Tough stuff can keep on happening, but
it's not because you're a bad person...it's
just the way of life.

The thing is, while you're sitting around
waiting, your life is passing you by. There

are already some really great things happening in your life — are you in a place to notice them?

When big, bad stuff happens, we look for equally big, good things, like lottery wins and holiday give-a-ways. However, it's better to start noticing the small stuff: the little things you maybe take for granted, the little gems that are buried among the everyday. These gems, when noticed, polished, and put on display, can form a collection that suddenly gives your life happiness again.

Notice the good things, big and small.
Notice what you have already.
Notice what is working. Notice who is still there. Notice what you love and like.

Life is what you notice. Notice the good things, and pay less attention to the bad things. Keep your focus firmly fixed on noticing beautiful things.

Life is also what you make it.

Don't wait for your ship to come in…swim

out there to meet it.

Plan good things. Plan opportunities for fun and more will come your way. Plan opportunities for joy and more joy will come your way.

Good things will flow to you mostly when good things are already happening. Plan them.

And if bad stuff or tough times come your way again, it's not because you did something wrong in a past life, or that the Universe is punishing you. It just so happens that life contains a mixture of good and bad.

Read this next line very carefully...

You are not cursed.

Good things *will* come your way again. They are already here. Be in a place where you can see them and appreciate them. Go looking for them. Set your lens to focus on everything good (big and small) and you'll quickly develop a life filled with joy and meaning.

So,

Step One
Plan Help
- Who are you going to see to help you with this?
- Where can you start?

Step Two
Plan and notice good things.
- What simple good things can you plan to do that will make your life better right now?
- Include daily, weekly, and monthly treats for yourself. (Use the hints from Chapter 5, and remember the best things in life are free).

Find good quality
people who are
just as dedicated
to helping you
as you are.
Find what and
whom you need
and give them
to yourself.

Conclusion

I have a confession to make.

This isn't actually the first book I started writing.

It's funny how when life starts to suck and tough times are thrown at you, the importance of things change.

I had started writing what I thought was a much-needed book on self-acceptance. So many of my clients come to me wanting to make changes or achieve their dreams and goals when deep down, the reason they can't do that on their own is because they get in their own way. They literally prevent themselves from having the life they want. Many of them have plenty of confidence, but not in the areas they need it most.

Deep down, they simply don't feel good enough. I wanted more than anything to help with this.

When my youngest daughter, Caterina, developed crippling pain, writing and focusing on helping others to achieve deep acceptance just didn't quite go together. That book had to wait.

Late last year when things were getting better and we finally began to put things behind us, I started to write again. I even utilized the support of a writing coach to help me through.

We were only a few short weeks into the process when two major things happened that shook my world to the core once again.

The first thing involved my eldest daughter, Mae. She had a major breakdown from all the stress she experienced seeing her little sister (and best friend) go through so much. They were so close, so it affected her greatly. She was also battling those early teenage years where nothing is easy. Remember those? (shudder)

Even though my husband and I tried so hard to be there for her at every stage, in the end that's actually impossible. It's hard to feel included and supported when you're doing all your high school assignments from a hospital corridor. It's hard to reach out and talk about your problems at school when all your teenage drama pales in comparison to someone else suffering severe health problems and pain.

Mae did what I've warned all of you not to in the first chapter. She turned on herself. And, of course, everything got worse.

(Insert depression here)

In the very same week, my nanna had a heart attack. She survived, but not without complications. Her lung function was also compromised, so between her heart and her lungs she now struggled with every single breath she took. Old age can be so cruel.

Those tough times got even tougher again.

Dear Life,
Thank you for sucking a bit more. Just
what I needed (not).
TM

When tough times happen, it really makes you count your blessings. It helps you put into focus those important things in life instead of the superficial things we get caught up in trying to attain. Suddenly we see the real value in genuine connections with people who love and support us, and we start to recognize that true beauty is found in nature and the world around us rather than shiny objects.

However, when harrowing, tough times happen, quickly followed by more and more tough times, it goes even deeper than that.

It makes you stop in your tracks and reassess your whole outlook on life. It either breaks you or it makes you.

That's the place I was at when I wrote this book.

I've always known who I am and what I love doing most in life, which is helping others get through things. I've always found that no amount of training I've had can compare to using the power of my own experiences to assist other people.

I'm already a great trauma coach, because I know what it's like to deal with trauma.

So when I was reassessing my life and pondering the deepest meanings behind it, I found myself wanting an even stronger purpose. I wanted even more meaning from an already meaningful life.

I asked myself: "What do I want my life to really be about?"

I knew these experiences, as horrible as they were, would help me help others. That's when I realized I didn't just want to help a handful of people; I wanted to help as many people as I possibly could.

Bit tricky when your clinic is already full.

I started to realize something powerful, something that had been right in front of me the whole time. When we go through something huge, our ability to be there for others increases. That means not only was I helping myself and my clients, but my clients would also go on to help others too.

Every person who has survived and thrived a sucky period of life are the best qualifiers for helping others who are going through a sucky life.

Think about it. It feels so supportive when we're at rock bottom and our friends say, *"Hang in there. It will get better, you'll see."*

And we want to believe them. We really do, but we're cynical.

However, think of the difference it makes when a close friend of ours sees us at a low point and gently says, "Remember when my mother had cancer, and my husband was out of work? I was in such a bad place. I cried every day. I know just how you feel right now... *but hang in there. It will get better, you'll see.*"

Same line, so much more meaning.

Of course I want you to be happy within. I'll still write that book but more than anything, I want you to first find that place that leads you to what's important to you.

What do you want your life to really be about?

That's where we find passion and purpose. That's when we find trust and confidence. That's when we crush fears. That's when we get out of our own way. That's also when we turn our lives around for the better.

Spend some time thinking about the following statement:

Imagine what your life will be like when you're living the life that is more aligned to your deepest desires.

You have learned all the steps needed to make this dream a reality.

You've learned to get behind yourself and be the support you need. You've called upon the incredible force of your survival mechanism. You've learned to process what's happening in ways that serve you, and avoid creating baggage. You've begun to utilize the benefits of journaling and mantras to help you move forward.

You've learned the importance of letting go of the things you can't control, and to take charge and authority over the things you can control, including your thoughts. You've learned to focus on the outcomes you desire, and you are moving forward.

You've hopefully begun to plan and enjoy wonderful things right here and now, so *today* is already better and not-so-sucky. You now understand how your past files can affect you now, and you know how to dissolve those patterns that are keeping you stuck.

You understand there are stages, and you can use the strengths of where you're at to help you get to the other side. You know how to watch out for emotions that create baggage. You know how to build a bridge right over it.

You've discovered the powerlessness being a victim creates, and learned to step into something much more empowering — *surviving*! This sets you up to *thrive* afterwards. You've learned there is always retribution for people who have wronged you, so you can let go of needing others to pay. You've learned what you need to do (the plan), and whom you can call on to help you find a way out.

I am so proud of you!

I know things are hard for you now, but I also know you can completely turn the whole thing around and have an extraordinary life.

But...

I also know that in order for this to be true

for you, you have to apply what you've learned.

Hopefully, your resource kit is nicely filled out and you can reflect on how far you've come. If you haven't utilized the resource kit, then don't forget to download it from my website.

Visit: www.tayamicola.com/resourcekit

You picked this book up for a reason. You read the title and something in it resonated with you. Although you have all the information you need to get through or over this, you may be looking for more help.

If you need more specific help, or some hand-holding, you can book in for a private session with me by visiting: www.tayamicola.com/book-now.

With all my love and compassion,

- Taya Micola

Imagine what
your life will
be like when
you're living
the life that is
more aligned
to your deepest
desires...

Acknowledgments

It actually takes more than one person to write a book.

Go figure.

First, I need to thank my book coach, Tracie McLee, who gave so much of her time to help get me started on this journey, and who taught me it can be done.

To my book writing buddies, Brenda and Saoirse, two amazing authors walking their own book-writing journeys, who spoke to me from across the globe each and every single week via Skype. Saoirse in particular stayed up very late just to work with my Australian time table, but both of you have no idea just how very much your love and support helped me make it all the way to the end of this book-writing caper.

To all the wonderful people in my mastermind community who gave so much of their time to help answer my technical questions, offered design feedback and shared all their incredible wisdom. Thank you.

To my awesome editor Beth Balmanno, whose patience, sage advice and wisdom has made editing my first book an incredibly positive experience. Thank you, Beth!

To my amazing web developer and long time bestie, Kym. Your support over the last 20 years in every step of my business and life has been immeasurable. Your incredible business advice and help in all things technical, despite my crazy, hair-brained, impractical schemes, is something I thank the Universe for every day. Thank you for taking my ideas and making them a reality. I am so blessed to have you in my life.

To my beautiful besties (Norelle, Angela, Kym and Shelley) and all my incredible friends (you know who you are) who were there for us with unwavering support during the hardest times in our life. I am forever indebted to you.

To my Mum, Dad, and sister for always encouraging me to go for anything I set my heart on. To Nanna for always believing in me.

To my amazing husband and our girls, for putting up with and supporting my crazy writing schedule as well as being my three greatest supporters.

And lastly but most importantly, the biggest thanks of all goes to my incredible clients and community. Your amazing journeys and drive for a better life inspire me to be a better therapist each and every day. It's a privilege to work with you and I have learned so much about your magnificence and the magnificence of the human spirit.

Can You Help Me?

If you enjoyed this book, could you PLEASE leave me a review on Amazon?

For any book to be successful, reviews—good or bad—play a big part. It would mean the world to me if you could take two minutes to leave an honest review.

Thank you so much, from the bottom of my heart!

Let's Connect

I'd love to connect more with you. Please reach out at any of the following:

Website:
www.tayamicola.com

Facebook:
@TayaMicolacom

Instagram:
@tayamicola

To find out about Taya's future books, visit:
www.tayamicola.com/upcomingbooks

About the Author

Taya Micola is a lover of life.
Born in Zimbabwe, Taya's family
immigrated to Australia (with nothing but
a small suitcase each) in the early 1980's.
Her family's "we can do this" motto taught
her that survival against all odds was
more dependent on attitude and self-belief

than skill itself.

Her devotion for helping others is only surpassed by her desire to enable others to powerfully help themselves.

With a passion for treating trauma, and helping those aspiring to create change in their lives - Taya offers therapy appointments in Kinesiology and Clinical Hypnotherapy in person from her clinic in Brisbane, Australia, or via Skype worldwide.

CPSIA information can be obtained
at www.ICGtesting.com
Printed in the USA
LVOW12s2232130417
530816LV00001B/135/P